T0194317

Her Toolbox

Learning to be a Female Leader
with Advice from Women in Power

ISHA UPPALAPATI

HER TOOLBOX
LEARNING TO BE A FEMALE LEADER WITH ADVICE FROM WOMEN IN POWER

Copyright © 2020 Isha Uppalapati.

All rights reserved. No part of this book may be used or reproduced by any means, graphic, electronic, or mechanical, including photocopying, recording, taping or by any information storage retrieval system without the written permission of the author except in the case of brief quotations embodied in critical articles and reviews.

iUniverse books may be ordered through booksellers or by contacting:

iUniverse
1663 Liberty Drive
Bloomington, IN 47403
www.iuniverse.com
844-349-9409

Because of the dynamic nature of the Internet, any web addresses or links contained in this book may have changed since publication and may no longer be valid. The views expressed in this work are solely those of the author and do not necessarily reflect the views of the publisher, and the publisher hereby disclaims any responsibility for them.

Any people depicted in stock imagery provided by Getty Images are models, and such images are being used for illustrative purposes only. Certain stock imagery © Getty Images.

ISBN: 978-1-6632-0680-0 (sc)
ISBN: 978-1-6632-0681-7 (e)

Library of Congress Control Number: 2020914790

Print information available on the last page.

iUniverse rev. date: 09/01/2020

To all the women leaders who supported me through this project and contributed to this book: I could not have done this without you, and I hope to make you proud.

Contents

Introduction ix

Stand Out 1

Your Foundation 9

Your Circle 16

Overcoming Adversity 23

Discipline 30

Learn to Fail 35

Thank You 40

Introduction

THE FUTURE IS OPEN TO ENDLESS POSSIBILITIES. Anything you want to do, you can do it. In a world full of opportunities, take control of your life, and make the best of everything you have.

You may feel stuck in an unfair situation, or you may be struggling to identify the next steps for your life. I wrote this book for girls in all stages of life: those who feel hopeless, those who are just getting started, and those who are rising fast. This book is to help young girls know they are not alone. We are all fighting various battles, and we can win. To create this book, I spoke to prominent female leaders from many different career paths with vastly different stories. I wanted to hear their histories and to understand their paths to success. This book is a reflection of their narratives, and it contains the best advice they had to offer.

The questions I asked revolved around three main topics: challenges, success, and advice. Although my conversations with each woman differed, there were a few questions I made sure to ask each female leader:

- What was your biggest challenge?
- What advice would you give to young girls?
- What is your passion?

The responses I received were extremely varied, but there were often common themes in many of the interviews. The different perspectives I received from each woman enhanced my knowledge and provided amazing content for me to share.

Before you get started, meet the women who are my inspiration and may become yours as well.

Freda Lyon is the Vice President for Emergency Services at Wellstar Health System, the largest health system in Georgia. She is the director of ten Emergency Departments, including the second-largest trauma center in the country. She was originally a nurse who was recognized for her sharp mind and ability to speak out and began to rise into leadership positions. She is an extremely well-educated woman and has always been an avid learner; furthermore, she is extremely qualified as a DNP, MSN, RN, and NE-BC. Freda Lyon was adopted by two wonderful parents and grew up in Phenix City, Alabama. Now, she has two successful kids and adorable grandchildren as well.

Anne Russel Bazzel is a vice president of the investment management division at Goldman Sachs. She is a successful woman in an industry that is mostly dominated by men. Her dedication and hard work have gotten her incredibly far. She went to William and Lee University for her bachelor's degree, majoring in Business and French, and received her MBA from Emory University. Growing up, Anne Bazzel was the middle child to two sisters, which made her independent from a young age. This independence helped her thrive and built the foundation for her to grow. Now, she has two daughters, ages two and four.

Dr. Melissa Rhodes is a pulmonary critical care doctor who built her own private practice with multiple doctors. Because of her hard work and determination, she was able to couple entrepreneurship with her passion for medicine. From a young age, Dr. Rhodes knew she wanted to be a doctor, and she associates her incredible skillset with her hard work and the morals her family taught her. She is the youngest of six kids, and she was raised in Gary, Indiana. During her childhood, her father owned and managed the family bar, and she and her siblings would often help out. This was the start of her enduring work ethic that she built on as she grew up. After graduating from the Indiana University School of Medicine (IU), Dr. Rhodes worked at other medical practices until she started her own.

Jana Kolarik is a partner and attorney with Foley & Lardner LLP. She is extraordinarily successful as a partner in a large international law firm. Mrs. Kolarik was inspired to go into healthcare law by her parents, who had professions in the medical field. Her focus on health care law, specifically compliance issues, started after her law school concentration in health law at the University of Maryland School of Law (UMD). Although she dabbled in a few other types of law before graduating from law school, Jana Kolarik has focused solely on health law in her career. Today, Mrs. Kolarik has a beautiful family and two kids.

Jill Rowley is a limited partner and fund advisor at Stage 2 Capital; however, she has had a very diverse career path. After graduating from the University of Virginia (UVA), she has spent time in management consulting, software sales, public speaking, growth advisory at Marketo, and then finally settled at Stage 2 Capital. At each venture, Mrs. Rowley learned something, whether her experience was good or bad. She has a passion for startups and growth, and always thrives on change. She is always willing to speak out. She has four kids and a wonderful family.

Philippa Ellis is the assistant general counsel at the Home Depot. She is the co-founder of an Atlanta law firm, and she recently transitioned to a new position at The Home Depot. When she was younger, Mrs. Ellis' passion was teaching. Although she initially went into college with plans to become an educator, her vision changed, and she wanted to become a lawyer. Although she was no longer going to be a teacher, Philippa Ellis' love for teaching was evident in her work. As a trial lawyer, she taught the jury about her case, and now at Home Depot, she has an abundance of training opportunities to help teach and mentor. Not only does she have a law degree from the University of Oklahoma College of Law, but she is also an MBA from the University of Georgia (UGA). She has two teenage twins, a boy and a girl.

Shyroll Morris is the vice president of Oncology and Gastroenterology at Wellstar Health System. She recently moved to Atlanta from the University of Miami for a better opportunity in her career. When Shyroll Morris was a young girl, she and her family immigrated from

Jamaica. Growing up, her parents were very busy, so she had to take the responsibility to help with her two younger sisters. She has always loved learning, carrying that passion with her every single day. Shyroll Morris did her undergrad at the University of Florida (UF) and got her MPH from University of South Florida (USF) and her MBA from Florida Atlantic University (FAU). She is also an avid biker and hiker.

All these women have been through challenges of their own, and they have emerged stronger and smarter. They share the advice that took them years to learn so other young women can learn from their decisions and succeed.

Right now, you may feel like you are stuck or that you will never improve your situation. These women that have climbed up this ladder already, and they are reaching down to pull you up. Never be afraid to ask for help. The world is full of people ready to give back as a way of thanking those who helped them. This book is to help you discover that you are not alone. The female leaders in this book want to see you soar and use their experiences and lessons to help guide your own success.

Stand Out

IT IS SO IMPORTANT TO BE IN CHARGE OF YOUR OWN LIFE, especially when it comes to your self-perception. You are often kinder to others than you are to yourself. However, in the same way, you can see the strengths and talents in others, you should be able to see within yourself.

Being independent is all about teaching yourself. This includes solving problems on your own and knowing when you need to ask for help. It is often hard for kids when parents watch over them and seem to be there constantly, but learning how to do things for yourself, even things as simple as making appointments and learning to advocate for yourself is the beginning of success. When I spoke with Anne Bazzel, she emphasized the importance of being in the driver's seat of your own life. She knew she would be financially independent after college, which steered the rest of her life. She put herself through grad school while working a full-time job. As a woman entering finance from a small liberal arts school that did not even have a finance major, Mrs. Bazzel knew there would be gaps in her education once she started working. After a few years on the job, she noted the gaps and realized the only way she would be able to be as good as she could be at her job would be to bridge those. She attended school several nights a week while again working full time to go to a senior-level finance course. Because she took the initiative to go back to school and learn the topics that made her feel less effective, she was able to succeed later. She took her learning into her control and realized if she did not fix what she did not know, she might always be behind.

You are in control of your future, and you have to make sure that you are living for yourself. It may be hard because people may be disappointed in the choices you make, but you must always make the decisions that benefit you. As I talked with these amazing women, I learned about the experiences that taught them to put themselves and their interests first. Dr. Melissa Rhodes explained how she always stuck to her work. Diligence is one of her most significant values, and she works to live up to it. For instance, Dr. Rhodes understood that this meant making difficult decisions like abandoning prior commitments. After medical school, she planned to complete her residency at the University of Virginia Medical School (UVA) to become a neurologist. However, before she could begin her residency, she had to do a general intern year. During this time, she realized her heart and her mind were in critical care. She loved neurology, and she loved her mentors who encouraged her path to UVA, but she decided that loving what she was going to do for the rest of her life was more important. Dr. Rhodes told me, "What I have tried to tell students is that you have to remember that it is your career, and you have to do something you love." She understood that it would be more difficult to find a new residency in her chosen career path, but she knew she was doing it for herself. Because of her passion and diligence, she is an incredibly successful woman today.

Being independent creates a work ethic; it encourages you to be able to fend for yourself. You learn to support yourself, and you teach yourself new skills along the way. You are willing to take bigger risks because you can make the jump without holding someone's hand.

Following a path for someone else will never bring you joy. It often brings regret because you will always be thinking of what you actually wanted to do. Freda Lyon told me her biggest regret was not taking a full ride to the University of Alabama at Birmingham (UAB) because her husband did not want to go with her. She passed up an incredible opportunity for her that she earned with hard work because of someone else. On the other hand, Jana Kolarik said the most difficult choice she ever had to make was to go to law school. Quitting her full-time job to be a full-time student again seemed terrifying. Everyone always told her how scary and hard it would be. Movies often portrayed law school as a horrific experience, but she resolved to go. She does not regret this decision and although choosing to get another degree was the hardest choice she ever made, it was also the best decision she ever made.

We are all scared of disappointing the people who have supported us, the people we look up to, and even the people who are our peers. However, we should never disappoint ourselves to satisfy someone else. In reality,

≈

if what you are doing is truly the best option, people are supportive. People often update their Linkedin, a common networking site in the business world, when they change jobs. Their former colleagues often flood the comments with praise, gratitude, and support. Jill Rowley says the best companies "applaud you when you leave." The people that you should care about will be supportive if you make the right decision for yourself.

Never be afraid to stand out or speak out because of what someone else may think because, for change to happen and to make a difference, people need to be uncomfortable. As Jill Rowley said, "You have to be comfortable with being uncomfortable." Getting out of your comfort zone is one of the hardest things to do, but it is 100% worth it." Freda Lyon said, "I think that part of diversity is allowing the tension. The differences are what make us better. If you do not have anyone challenging the opinion that is on the table, then nothing will ever change." If you try to conform and try to act like someone else, you may never succeed. There already is that someone else; you need to stand out and be yourself.

When you stand out, people notice you. When this happens, they are more willing to help you. People are always scared that, when they embark on a new journey, they will be alone. You may not receive support from your close family or friends, but you are not alone. People are almost always more than willing to help if they see your efforts. While we often focus on the bad people most people are good. They want to help you succeed and thrive, but they are only willing to help someone who is special, unique, and true to themselves. Therefore, if you are pretending to be someone that you are not, you may find yourself alone.

The most important thing to remember is that you have to be passionate about what you do. Every empowering woman that I talked to emphasized the importance of passion. Jill Rowley says, "If you are not passionate about it, if it is not something you are excited to do, if you are not working with people that you respect and share the same values, you are going to be miserable, and ultimately that will catch up with you." You only live once, so spend your time doing something that you love. If you are passionate about something, you will be more willing to pursue excellence at your chosen task. To be a leader, the top of a field, or an inspiration to others, you need to be doing something you love. Jill Rowley told me when she was at UVA, she picked the major that she thought would get her the best job because that is what she wanted. Instead of majoring in subjects she loves, like marketing or management, she majored in finance. In reality, she did not want to work on Wall Street. She did not even want to work in investment banking. She realized she would never be happy working in finance, so she transitioned to a sales position. As a competitive person, sales was her home. She fought to always be on the top of the leaderboard, proving to herself and everyone around her that this is where she belonged.

Your passion can also change. As you grow and mature, so may your dreams. Freda Lyon said she originally wanted to be a neonatologist, but after having a child, she realized that was not what she wanted. She still wanted to be able to help people, so she became a nurse. Throughout her career, her passion for helping people never left. She said, "If I'm the director of an emergency department that sees 60,000 patients, then I've impacted 60,000 lives. And if I have a staff of a hundred, I've impacted all hundred of those lives." Even as she grew, that seed that bloomed into her dream remained the same, even though her career path changed, Shyroll Morris's dream, when she was 13 years old, was to become a hospital administrator. A close family friend told her, "that is not a good idea, those people get fired almost every other day." Unfortunately, this friend was a nurse who saw a lot of change in hospital administration, and Shyroll believed her perspective. Yet years later, Shyroll became the director of oncology and gastroenterology of the WellStar Health System. Even though she explored many careers and pursued different paths, she chose a career that reflected her true passion.

As much as it can guide people towards success, passion alone cannot make you successful. Melissa Rhodes says, "It is important to have a passion for what you do and discipline, but you cannot achieve anything, whatever it is, whether it is a class that you are taking or a book that you are writing or a club that you want to get in or a test that you take, whatever it is, it is not just going to happen. You have to make it happen. You have to work to make it happen."

You have to be in the driver's seat. You have to be willing to put in the hard work. Anne Bazzel told me that "you hold the control; you are in the driver's seat of your life. There are going to be opportunities that happen to land in your lap, but for the most part, you are the one who is going to be creating opportunities for yourself. And you might not, you might actually create those opportunities, but the way that you build relationships throughout your career, the way you nurture those relationships, the way you give freely of your time, whether that is in the business world or the academic world, or whether that is among your friends, the way that you give can be how you should expect to receive sort of opportunities." Nothing comes without hard work, and you have to learn that you are the only person that can make you successful.

You have to be able to form your own opinions, which is especially challenging in the age of social media. Everyone is always connected, so sometimes it is hard to come up with your own opinions. Jana Kolarik explains, "You have to have enough perspective on your own to put aside the things that are not worth paying attention to and then pulling in the things that you know are worth paying attention to." If your opinions are all based on what someone else says or thinks, you are trying to be someone else, but if your opinions and ideas stand out, you are more likely to become a leader by being an independent thinker. What's more, you stand out and are the best version of yourself. Leaders should not blend in. Their voices should be loudly and clearly heard.

Do not be afraid to speak out. If you feel that something needs to change, be honest, and try to make a change happen. People may not always agree with you, but, at the end of the day, do what you think is right. During Jill Rowley's time at Oracle, she identified flaws and reported them to company executives. Many of them did not take it too well or did not agree with her perspective, and she was eventually let go. Jill Rowley never took that as an indictment of her excellence., Instead, she recognized it as a sign that the company was not the right fit for her. Consequently, she moved on to her next opportunity, which was a much better fit for her in the end. Freda Lyon reaped the benefits of speaking out. As an ER nurse, she regularly spoke her mind on what needed to change. She's the type of person who "when she sees something she says something." Her initiative and courage were rewarded: she began being offered management positions and eventually worked up to VP of Emergency Services at Wellstar.

You have to be able to stand up for yourself. Even if you are the smartest, most deserving person in the room, no one will know unless you speak up. Although someone may be the most deserving person to receive something, Jill Rowley says, "You do not get what you deserve. You get what you negotiate." Unless you are willing to speak up and make your voice heard, you will never get what you deserve. Do not tell yourself or anyone else that you cannot do this because you are a woman. After all, being a woman should never stop you. You have a unique perspective on the world that many male peers may not have, and you should embrace that uniqueness. Being the only one of your gender, race, or age does not mean you should not do it. If anything, use that individuality as a strength: always stand out.

Your Foundation

According to Shyroll Morris, there are three building blocks for a successful future: education, experience, and mentors.

These three things compose your foundation; they are the most important tools to success and the basis for your resume and career. These priorities closely interact with one another. We gain education from experience and mentors; We gain experience from education; and we gain mentors from education and experience.

In today's business environment, post-secondary education is often a prerequisite for leadership positions. It boosts your resume and makes you more prepared for a higher-level job. Ms. Morris said that, because of her additional Master's degree, she was qualified for more ambitious positions. When she applied for a position as the Chief Operating Officer at a company, she competed with highly-qualified candidates, including a former Chief Financial Officer., He was a more experienced c-suite candidate, but she said her "extra degrees gave her an edge," allowing her to demonstrate her knowledge, experience, and cultural fit for the position. In other words, educational credentials make a difference. Another inspiring woman, Freda Lyon, started as a nurse working in emergency settings. Soon she began to rise through the ranks because she always spoke out, but as she continued to higher-level positions, Freda Lyon knew her education had to support her occupation. Although she started her career as an LPN, a licensed practical nurse, and now she has multiple degrees, including a doctorate in nursing.

Education is an ongoing endeavor. it is not just about classroom teaching; rather, it is the place where lifelong learners are formed. As Satya Nadella, the CEO of Microsoft, says, " Do not be a know-it-all; be a learn-it-all." Never stop learning. Anne Bazzel went back to school after she was already working a full-time job because she wanted to continue to learn. Philippa Ellis went back to get her MBA because she wanted to learn about a new aspect of her industry while already being a successful lawyer. Jana Kolarik left her job and attended law school because she knew her education would lead to greater opportunities. Of course, learning also does not always happen in a classroom. We learn from our peers and from our own successes and mistakes. Dr. Melissa Rhodes emphasized the importance of the love of learning and reading. Loving to read opens up so many opportunities because, as Jill Rowley says, "If you can see it, you can be it." Reading opens up so many different paths because you can learn about a new career, find someone that inspires you, and even see a future for yourself that you may never have seen before. Dr. Rhodes reiterates this idea, saying, "The love of reading is such a core to our education and not just reading in school but reading at home and reading all different things to expand your mind because then you can learn of possibilities and that the possibilities are endless, but you cannot start that without opening your mind and learning about things and wanting to have the love of learning." She has always carried that love of learning with her throughout her life. She knew she wanted to go to attend quality schools, but as a child, her parents were unable to pay for her to continue going to a private school for high school. She started her own newspaper route, working while going to high school and all of summer, to pay for her high school education. She had 70 houses on her route, and would always let them know when she would be coming by or if there would be a change in when the paper got dropped off. She learned skills on how to communicate with people, especially regarding money. During college, she continued to work during the year and throughout the summer. One year, she was working in Northern Virginia while staying with her brother during the summer because she knew she could make more money there than at home. She did not have a car, so she took the bus to the train station to go to DC before walking 30 minutes from the train station to her first job. At the end of her workday, she would leave for her second job before finally arriving home around midnight. Education is not always easy, but with commitment and perseverance, she achieved her goal. She understood how important it was for her to get a good education, and with her hard work to fund her future, she learned skills that cannot be learned in the classroom. Dr. Rhodes learned the importance of discipline, and her hard work gave her experience.

Experience is a critical building block of long-term success because you learn skills by working with other people. The experience you gain from education is often more important than the topics themselves. During Philippa Ellis' MBA, she often learned more from her peers than her professors. Dr. Rhodes also spoke about the importance of her experience in medical school: "People want to shorten it, but I do not think it should be because I think it needs to be logged to experience, to have so many different experiences where somebody is watching out over you to teach you and to guide you and to see where you are going and to make a mistake and then learn from that." Going to school is analogous to learning how to ride a bike: when you are first starting, you need someone to hold your bike and have training wheels to learn the basic motion, but soon, someone lets go and the training wheels come off. There was something to catch you, allowing you to make a mistake, but never allowing you to fall. Going to school and having the support of your peers and professors are like training wheels, and that support allows you to learn the skills needed to succeed. Learning from your mistakes will make you extremely successful. Do not consider each mistake a failure; instead, each mistake is a learning opportunity from which you can grow. Freda Lyon told me that she "learns more from her mistakes than her successes." Each mistake made provides an opportunity to evaluate the situation and see all the other options that would have been successful so you do not make the same mistake twice. Each experience is a learning opportunity to change something that went wrong and to become a better person, whether it is professionally or personally.

Shyroll Morris said that education gives you so much experience in such little time. In no other setting would you be with so many people of the same or similar caliber as you, all willing and eager to learn. Everyone wants to explore new concepts, and they also want to share what they know. The experience of education gives you lifelong advice on communication, negotiation, and friendships. You can find any mentors through education, as well. Anne Bazzel was greatly influenced by a professor that helped her become as successful as she is today. After her semester abroad in southern France, Mrs. Bazzel returned, wanting to change her major from economics to business. Her new goal was to go into finance after an incredibly life-changing experience in France. She immersed herself in the culture as she was fluent in the language and felt it was impactful to step out of her comfort zone. She advocates for kids to step out of their comfort zone and participate in a semester abroad. If you go to another country and experience a different lifestyle, you are so much more prepared to step into life with multiple perspectives. You can use your experiences from a different place to advise on how something could be more efficient or to build deeper relationships with people who have experienced similar cultures. Once Anne Bazzel returned from her semester abroad and took a few finance classes, she realized that was the path she wanted to go for her career. Changing your major senior year is extremely difficult since you have to take a lot more classes to fulfill major requirements, but Anne Bazzel knew what she wanted, so she worked hard to graduate as a double major in business and French. To accomplish this, she asked her finance professor for help. Her professor helped her prepare for interviews for investment banks, and through that hard work and discipline, she got job offers from the same places that hired people who had been doing finance for four years at prestigious institutions. The help of her education, her experience in France, and the mentorship from her finance professor were the building blocks to the start of her career.

Shyroll Morris also stressed the importance of solidifying your foundation. If your foundation is weak or not sufficient enough for a certain career, you may fall short of expectations. Never be too scared to take a leap and try for a new opportunity, but if you cannot fulfill your new role, it is incredibly difficult to get back up. By starting with a strong foundation, you will eliminate any doubts that people have of your capabilities because you are better prepared to meet or exceed their expectations.

The most significant component of your foundation is your mindset. Look at each opportunity to work towards your dreams. Keep yourself receptive to the advice and opportunities that come your way so you can take advantage of any situation. That's why Dr. Rhodes encourages girls, "to open up their mind to the limitless possibilities and to work hard so that the world is your oyster." Use each experience, whether good or bad, as a learning opportunity to grow. There will be obstacles along the way, but you can overcome them with hard work and the skills you learn from education, experience, and mentors. After you lay a solid foundation, the future you build will be nearly indestructible.

Your Circle

PEOPLE WANT TO HELP. THERE ARE TWO PARTS OF YOUR circle: your support system and mentors. First, your support system consists of your family and friends. Having a supportive family is one of the most significant blessings you can have. If your family is lacking, you can make up for that with friends. Dr. Melissa Rhodes credits her parents for being supportive and instilling her with morals that she embraces to this day. Their nurture helped her develop traits that have made her a hard worker and independent woman. She highly respects her parents, who fully supported her endeavors. As she continued to grow, her husband became one of her most prominent supporters. She believes the support from her home life has been foundational to her success. Support can come in different forms, including financial and moral. Moral support encourages you to believe in yourself and help you realize your true potential. However, if you are faced with an unsupportive family, overcoming that makes you a stronger person. Philippa Ellis talked about how some members of her extended family were unsupportive of her choice to go to law school. They told her many people are lawyers and that she would have a hard time being successful in an already-saturated career field. Mrs. Ellis continued with her goal to become a lawyer, ignoring the naysayers to fulfill her dream. She knew whose advice to take - her parents, who supported her goal - and continued towards her path to success. By figuring which people are beneficial in your life, you can start to ignore those who do not support you or do not have your best interests in mind. For example, after Freda Lyon had her kids so early in her life, many close family and friends told her what she would never be able to achieve. By doing that, they motivated her even more so she could prove them wrong. By converting negative energy into motivation, you can take advantage of each situation to its fullest.

At times, it can be difficult to identify your support system. Especially as a young kid who desperately wants to fit in, trying to blend in with any group can be extremely enticing. Develop a habit of identifying which friends want the best for you. it is more important to have a few good ones than many mediocre ones who are self-interested.

As Jana Kolarik explains, "People always are important. And you will find people who were meaningful to your path at the time, and you learned something from, and then they fall away, and you grow apart or grow differently. But surrounding yourself with people who you care about and who care about you and who were supportive of you is good." There are times in your life when you need a certain type of friend. When developing your professional life, you may need someone who is connected to that career. Meanwhile, if you are focusing on your personal life, you may need someone who is more empathetic.

Friendships are not transactional. You can count favors and expect to get something every time you give. Jill Rowley likes to say: "Give to give; do not give to get." Make sure your relationship is not one-sided. If you are always giving to another person, you may soon be worn down. Instead, strive for mutually-supportive relationships. There are three kinds of symbiotic relationships: parasitism, commensalism, and mutualism. In parasitic relationships, one animal benefits from the other animal at the other animal's expense. In a commensalistic relationship, one animal benefits from the other without the other being harmed or helped. Finally, mutualism is the most favorable relationship: both animals benefit from each other, and neither is harmed. You want most of your friendships to be mutualistic so both parties are better off with the relationship. If you are the only one benefiting from a relationship, the other person may distance themselves because it is not worth the time and love they are putting in if they are getting nothing back. Known as parasitic relationships, these friendships are draining. Stay away and try to leave those as soon as possible; they do far more harm than good.

Second, always make connections, which may prove to be even more helpful than personal experiences. If you have a trustworthy relationship with people, you will have a new world of opportunities. Jill Rowley spoke of an experience where a brief acquaintance asked for a referral to the Chief Marketing Officer (CMO) of a certain company. This acquaintance had a weak relationship with Mrs. Rowley, yet she still requested a job referral. Mrs. Rowley was not willing to risk her reputation on a person she barely knew. However, had this woman built a solid relationship with Mrs. Rowley prior to asking for a referral, she may have landed the job. Nurturing relationships is incredibly important. That's why Philippa Ellis identifies nurturing relationships with mentors as the most important piece of advice for young girls. Do not expect mentors to reach out to you. If someone offers their expertise or assistance, they are willing to give you as much time as possible. Take the initiative to reach out and grab as many opportunities as you can. Most people will go out of their way to help you because most people are inherently good. Anne Bazzel explained that "people want to help those who have potential." Do not shy away from showing people your true capabilities because, if people can see your full potential, they will respect you so much more.

Just like there are different friends for different times in your life, there are different mentors for different times as well. Depending on what you are looking at as the next step, choose a mentor wisely. For Philippa Ellis, there came a time in her life where she searched for a mentor who had kids to help better guide her. While she took on this new step in life, she wanted to see how others could do it and learn from their experiences. From those mentors, she learned how to maximize her time with her family while not sacrificing her career. As your goals and priorities change, you will find the people that are the most qualified to help you in each situation. But even as your priorities change, do not lose track of your mentors. Not only may their expertise be useful later, but they can also become a very good friend. As you progress through your career, the very same person who taught you so many of the skills that led to your success may come asking you for advice or help. For example, Ms. Morris and her former mentor continuously stayed in touch and checked with one another, but one day, Shyroll Morris hired one of the women who helped her journey. It was a long-term expression of a symbiotic relationship.

As a woman, it is important to get advice from other women. One of the deciding factors for Shyroll Morris to move from her position at the University of Miami to the Wellstar Health System was the fact that Wellstar's leadership team included many women. This ensured a possibility for growth and the opportunity to connect with and learn from many high-performing women. Many of Anne Bazzel's mentors were women. In addition, Philippa Ellis has mentored many young female lawyers by sharing her experiences.

Know the difference between mentors and advocates. As Anne Bazzel beautifully explains: "Mentors can come in different forms. A mentor is typically someone more experienced than you are who serves as a role model and will help you navigate the workplace and coach you through tricky situations. In some cases, mentors & mentees may be assigned. Other times, mentors develop more naturally. In my experience, mentors become friends and confidants who are willing to provide feedback, advice, and serve as a sounding board. Mentors provide career advice and leadership development. I think of mentors as close personal advisors.

Advocates are your champions. They are typically senior leaders within your organization who will advocate on your behalf for opportunities and advancement. Advocates can be senior leaders who take a personal interest in the future success of high potential teammates. Advocates can also help broaden your relationships within and outside of an organization. Importantly, advocates provide encouragement and help enlarge your sense of what you are capable of achieving."

Not all mentors have to be personal friends. Jill Rowley notes that books, podcasts, informational videos, or blogs can become a significant mentor in your life. Not knowing someone through your personal life does not mean they have not taught you important tools that have helped you succeed.

Remember that friends and mentors may come and go, but never forget the lessons they teach you. Whether you had a good or bad experience with them, you can learn just as much from their failures as you can from their successes. However, do not be scared to move on from a friend or a mentor if there is a greater opportunity. In the situation of leaving a company to go somewhere else, it may seem that you are leaving everyone behind, but in reality, you are just leaving the company; the people and friends who are there to support you will still be with you.

When Philippa Ellis left the law firm that she founded, she was hesitant because she had to leave behind so many people and experiences. But those experiences will never leave her because she will always remember the lessons learned from them. She also made sure her relationships were stable before she left and personally talked to all her clients to let them know of her pending departure and encourage them to stay with her former firm because, even though she was leaving, she had immense respect for the firm and did not want them to be harmed by a sudden loss of client due to her departure.

Your circle is a representation of yourself. These people should be a reflection of your values, pursuits, and intended perceptions. Being young, it is incredibly hard to find the right group of friends, and there are times when you may feel lonely, but you will find the people that support you through your endeavors and help cultivate your knowledge. They should have similar priorities and drive as you. Surround yourself with people that you admire.

Overcoming Adversity

You WILL FACE SO MANY CHALLENGES IN YOUR LIFE, and you must learn how to fight each battle. The challenges you face will vary. Some may be temporary, but others may continue for the rest of your life.

First, you should learn how to overcome outside bias caused by unfair stereotypes, including age, race, gender, and sexual preference. By disproving negative stereotypes, you have shown that you are an even stronger person than those who did not have to fight against that bias. The upward battle to fight a stereotype builds strength and character. As women, many of the successful leaders I interviewed have faced gender discrimination. Philippa Ellis recalls multiple moments where someone assumed she was a secretary when she walked into a courtroom, disregarding that she was dressed in a crisp suit with a briefcase and laptop. Prejudice has cost her status, respect, and opportunity. She encourages women to remain calm. Even though she did feel disrespected during these instances, she stayed poised and did not let her anger show. However, showing restraint does not mean you let people walk over you. Instead, pick and choose your battles. There will always be people who put you down because of something you cannot control. Jana Kolarik recalls a time when a former male employer told her that she would never become a lawyer and that she will never graduate from law school because of her gender. Mrs. Kolarik notes that it is incredibly important to have a strong sense of purpose and to not let other people's doubts or insecurities drive your decision making. Do not let doubters bring you down, and as Jana Kolarik says, "follow your heart, and trust your gut." Freda Lyon spoke about an experience where she was treated far differently than her male counterparts. As a female nurse in management, if she showed up to meetings in scrubs, she was often looked down upon or ignored, but male doctors or nurses wearing scrubs were not treated the same way. While Freda Lyon had to wear formal clothing during those meetings to command the respect she deserved, male doctors could stay in their scrubs and get the same respect. Although this was upsetting, Mrs. Lyon knew that she needed to choose her battles wisely. She wore professional business attire to her next meeting.

Of course, strong reactions are, at times, inevitable. For example, Mrs. Ellis recalled a situation at her first law firm. One of the senior partners of the firm was participating in inappropriate activities, and they directly affected Ms. Ellis. She gathered the courage to walk into his office and call him out on the immorality of what he was doing. She was direct and conveyed how she felt regarding the situation. Although she had done nothing wrong, it took a lot of courage to express herself like that, especially to the man who was her boss.

Circumstances can be challenging, but that does not mean that they do not present unique opportunities. For instance, Freda Lyon was married and pregnant in high school, which resulted in her displacement from school and years of marital struggle. She raised her daughter as she built her career, but Freda Lyon is the type of person to always find the silver lining. Her positive mindset radiated as she mentioned that she was lucky to have had her daughter, Angel, earlier than she would have planned because, as a result, her mom was able to meet her granddaughter. Mrs. Lyon's mother died two years after Angel was born, so Freda Lyon sees having her first child at such a young age as a blessing. By taking the best of every situation, you can consider each event as a step in a positive direction. That's why Jill Rowley advises you to "challenge yourself to assume the positive." By developing a positive mindset, you can envision all the good possibilities and strive to achieve one of your goals.

Of course, even good things come with challenges. Many of these amazing women I talked to have children of all ages. Children are a wonderful addition to a family, and many women dream of having kids. However, many women also fear a high-level career because they want to be present for their children, but it is completely possible to have both. Philippa Ellis talked about how she would take her kids to work with her and give up things like frequent manicures to spend more time with them. Anne Bazzel says she has become much more efficient since having kids so that she can be fully present after work. Balancing your work and personal life is a constantly shifting scale. As Jana Kolarik says, "there are times when your career will take the number one priority and then times when you and your family take the spot." That position can shift day-to-day, and it is important to know which one you should prioritize.

Having a personal life to relax from the stress of your job is crucial. For some people, it may be spending time with your family, and for others it may be exercise or art. For Shyroll Morris, biking and hiking are her outlets for stress. Some of her adventures include biking across Jamaica, biking to the Keys, and hiking to base camp on Mount Everest. One of her most notable experiences was her hike to the top of Mount Kilimanjaro. This hike not only showed off her athletic prowess and dedication but also her resilience. On her first attempt, she did not reach the top, but that did not stop her. Six months later, she returned and completed the hike, not allowing her initial failure to stop her from accomplishing her goal. These breaks from work allow you to be your best at work.

Sometimes, it is important to know where bias comes from. As Shyroll Morris says, "unfamiliarity causes a lot of adversity." Many people are unfamiliar with a culture, which makes them apprehensive because they are unsure of what to expect. Ms. Morris is an immigrant from Jamaica, and she said much of the discrimination she faced was not because of hatred for her nationality or race. Rather, people were unfamiliar with her culture. Using unfamiliarity as an excuse to judge someone else should not be supported, but it is important to remember that although you may seem prejudiced against, it is not always because someone does not like you.

You may have to adapt because of differentiating factors. For Jana Kolarik, she says that she markets herself a little differently as a woman. Her socializing opportunities and priorities are different. She puts a strong emphasis on client relationships and uses those relationships to network. Marketing herself differently does not make her any less of a lawyer, but it does emphasize her strongest traits.

Often overcoming adversity is a matter of perspective. That's why Dr. Melissa Rhodes challenges people to view difficult situations as challenges, not obstacles. While obstacles are often perceived as a more permanent boundary that you cannot cross, challenges are an opportunity to rise up to the situation and grow. Think of obstacles as a brick wall and a challenge as a hurdle. The only way to get through a brick wall is by breaking it down, which may be unachievable with the tools you have, but you can overcome a hurdle by having the strength and power to make the jump. It may take more than one attempt, but as long as you keep trying, you will grow and learn. Never let yourself be your biggest barrier. People, especially girls, doubt themselves, and that doubt prevents them from succeeding. Not believing in yourself causes you to erect artificial barriers. As a result, girls often do not apply for promotions, speak up, or embrace challenging projects.

One of Anne Bazzel's most significant challenges was a project assigned to her by her former firm. At large financial institutions, there is often little room for entrepreneurship without being an executive, but one day Mrs. Bazzel was given the opportunity to create her own group within the firm. This was her first time in a management role and being an entrepreneur, but she did not shy away from the challenge. No matter how frightening or difficult it may have been, Anne Bazzel worked through it and proved not only to others but also to herself that she excelled at this level. Although it was one of the hardest tasks she has embarked on, she also says it was one of the most incredible opportunities. As a woman in finance, Anne Bazzel is quite rare. She says that many women shy away from the financial services industry because of fear of failure or the fear they will not fit in. She never shied away from a challenge, and neither should you. Challenges do not impede success, and you can use your differences as an advantage to stand out.

There will be times when you feel like everything is in your way, but you have to persevere. Freda Lyon says:

> "You just push through and survive. You just got to get to this next semester. There's a two-week break in between the next semester. If I could just get there, you know, I'll be okay. It all works out. I've worked three jobs in my career, I had two babies, and I was a single parent. You just have to do what you have to do, so I worked a couple extra jobs. That's okay. You just have to do it."

Even while going to school and working multiple jobs, Freda Lyon had to take care of two young children, but she did not let that challenge stop her. She knew once she got past now, her future would look so much better. Do not let a temporary setback or challenge stop you from achieving your future.

Overcoming adversity is a critical component of long-term success. Whether navigating challenges associated with prejudice, capability, or opportunity, it is possible to achieve your desired outcome. Truly, challenges are an opportunity to become strong, more competent, and more ready to attain the life that you want.

Discipline

Iｆ ｙｏｕ ｔａｋｅ ｏｎｅ ｔｈｉｎｇ ａｗａｙ ｆｒｏｍ ｔｈｉｓ ｂｏｏｋ, ｉｔ should be the importance of hard work.

Even with all the right tools, a firm foundation, and supportive people, you will not be successful without hard work. Jill Rowley strongly believes, "you can be anything you want to be regardless of where you come from, but it takes a lot of hard work." By putting in hard work, you will be able to do anything you want.

Dr. Melissa Rhodes is a strong advocate for the importance of hard work. Her father became disabled during her childhood, before she went to high school, so her life changed drastically. For example, she had to pay her own tuition to her private Catholic high school on her own, and her mother had to work to replace her father's lost income. Even so, she said the one thing that never changed was the importance of hard work and education. Life's challenges can be overcome with hard work and knowledge. Regardless of your circumstances, continue to work hard. Identify the long-term rewards, and work hard to achieve your goals. If the people around you do not have the discipline that you want to carry with you, do not let that stop you. Through your experiences, you can learn what traits you do not want to carry with and work to move away from them. In this process, it helps to find mentors that can guide your development, and embody the same traits that you admire. For example, Jill Rowley had a goal to save one million dollars by the time she was 30. Her eagerness to save money does not come from her parents or her friends. Her father still works at 70 years old because he was not as cautious with saving his money. Jill Rowley realized how important it was to save and taught herself the important skills of personal finances to be prepared for the future. She accomplished her goal of saving that one million dollars and has now built an abundance of wealth that she can lean back on because of her discipline.

This principle reminds me of trying to ride a bike up a hill. When you are riding a bike up a hill, it may seem impossible to get to the top. You continue pedaling, but you still cannot see over the edge. If you stop putting in the strength to keep pedaling, you will fall, and restarting is nearly impossible. However, if you can keep pushing and putting in the hard work to reach the top, you can rest the entire way downhill. Use the break to regain the strength to push through the next challenge. Freda Lyon exhibits this principle. Working as a single mom with two school-aged kids, she realized the importance of pushing to the next break. Even if it was a short, one week break, she knew that pushing herself to that time would give her the opportunity to regroup and start the next semester or project with newfound energy and passion.

Developing the mindset to not give up should start

when you are young. Oftentimes, parents, relatives, and close friends instill you with morals that you will carry with you for the rest of your life. This was true for Dr. Rhodes, who grew up in a Catholic family and considers her Catholic faith very meaningful to her today. The morals she learned from her religion, teachers, and parents while growing up and attending Catholic school continue to inform her decision-making. Most notably, she learned the importance of discipline, which she allowed her to pay for her private high school and college. She gave up parties and social events to complete her school work, and have time for her job. Knowing that she would learn lessons that would help her succeed for the rest of her life, like managing and saving time and money, kept her motivated. Often, hard work is a long-term investment in your future.

You will want to work hard if you are pursuing a path that you are passionate about. After all of Jill Rowley's years of hard work, all her work still relates to her passion. Eventually, she gained financial independence, allowing her to quit at any time. Now, she works because she loves it. Because her job was not a chore, but something she wanted to do, she often exceeded expectations. The lesson is clear: do something you love, so that no matter how hard it gets, you can look at why you fell in love with it in the first place and use that passion as fuel to keep going.

Working hard is important, but make sure to find balance. Shyroll Morris worked incredibly hard the first ten years of her career, but one thing she would tell her younger self is to relax and enjoy life. She encourages you to always work hard, but also take time to enjoy yourself.

Now, Shyroll Morris bikes and hikes as a break from her career. Find balance or else you may overwork yourself and lose your passion. For example, many kids fall out of love with a sport they have played their entire lives because they didn't give themselves an opportunity to rest. Allow yourself time to relax so you remain passionate about your work.

There will come a time in your life to relax after your hard work has paid off. Jill Rowley is experiencing that in the summer of 2020. Even though she is not working in a traditional workplace setting, she is still pursuing her passion and change. She has more time to relax now after her years of hard work because she was disciplined to build a solid future where she does not need to be constantly working. When you are younger, your priorities build your future, so put in the work when you are young.

Having the ability to prioritize what needs more attention and effort will balance your life. Understanding what needs more time and resources will allow you to work more efficiently and get more done. Anne Bazzel is now incredibly efficient at work because of her kids. She prioritizes being present during dinner and bedtime, so she has found a way to be more efficient at work so she can accomplish her priorities. Freda Lyon realized she did a lot of things the hard way, and in hindsight, she admits her life may have been easier had she waited to have kids and get married until after she graduated college. Although she took the harder path, she still succeeded because she worked harder.

Extra effort can make up for many things, including intelligence, support systems, and experience. Anne

≈

Bazzel grew up with two sisters, both very successful and intelligent women. She admits that both of them were smarter than her, and she had to work much harder to do as well as them, but her work ethic paid off. Ultimately, you are the only judge of your effort. Publicly, you are measured by your results, and often your results are a reflection of your work ethic.

Hard work and discipline takes many forms. Work hard to make relationships that will support you for the rest of your career, work hard to create opportunities for yourself, and work hard to make an impact on those around you. Build the discipline to work hard and plan for your future by creating a set of standards to live by. Do something you love so you do not want to quit, and use that love and passion to fuel you to persevere towards your goals. If you are stuck in undesirable circumstances, hard work and passion will propel you towards your dreams.

Learn to Fail

THE FIRST THING YOU NEED TO LEARN HOW TO DO IS TO fail. You will fail so many times in your life that it is important to learn how to fail when you are young. Most importantly, allow failures to be learning opportunities. Anne Bazzel was the first person I ever heard say, "learn how to fail." The fear of failure stops you more than anything else. Therefore, she encourages people to take the hardest classes possible, even if it means not earning top marks in that course. Challenging yourself and getting out of your comfort zone will help you more than any grade ever will. Doubting yourself and not allowing yourself to try is a form of failure. Not succeeding is just an opportunity to try again and learn something new, a reality that Dr. Melissa Rhodes knows well. When she was in high school, she had to take an aptitude test that suggested a future career path. The results were not what she had hoped for, and a counselor told her that she would never be able to go into medicine. She did not let that one test dictate the rest of her life; rather, she used it as a learning opportunity. Dr. Rhodes did not let that one naysayer stand in the way of achieving her goals. She understood that just because she struggled with something at the beginning did not mean she would never be good at it. With her hard work and passion, she knew that she would be great.

What you consider failure is determined in your own mind. If you believe every time you make a mistake you have instantaneously failed, you will fail every day for the rest of your life, but if you consider each mistake as an opportunity for growth, you will be extraordinarily successful. Freda Lyon says, "you can do anything you set your mind to." If you can change your mindset to see the possibilities, you can achieve anything. At Anne Bazzel's first job, she felt as though she were behind compared to her other colleagues. She did not allow her gaps in her education to stand in her way. She did not consider those gaps as failures but as opportunities to improve, and with that mindset, she went to a high-level night school class to meet her expectations. Anne Bazzel committed to becoming more knowledgeable so she could be even better, and she did it, but the important thing to remember is she did it for herself. No one asked her to go to school, and no one said she was not good enough. She was her own motivation.

Do not let the fear of disappointing someone stop you from taking risks. Make sure to get out of your comfort zone to experience new cultures, see new ways of doing something, and expand your knowledge. Anne Bazzel went to France during college to immerse herself in the culture, and she spoke so highly of that experience that she encourages everyone to try to get out of their comfort zones. For Freda Lyon, she lost the opportunity to go to UAB on a full scholarship because her former husband did not want to get out of his comfort zone and leave their hometown. Getting out of your comfort zone, whether it is a good or bad experience, teaches you how to handle more versatile situations and have a higher chance of success.

"Know your why," Jill Rowley told me that during our conversation. People want to believe in a person that believes in their cause. People cannot believe in your abilities until they believe in your why. The most successful people, including all the women interviewed, do something worthy of their time and investment. To do something just for money or for another person will not make you successful as success is not defined by wealth. Unanimously, the women I interviewed said "success" meant being happy and helping others. If you are not content in what or why you do something, you will never be successful.

Jill Rowley also said, "Fall down seven times and get up eight." When climbing the ladder to success, each time you fall down a rung, make sure you get back up. However, unless you climb one more rung than the number you fell down, you will be in the same place you started. If your goal is to rise up the leadership ladder, then you have to climb further than where you started. Freda Lyon got up more than once. Before even starting her career, Mrs. Lyon had two kids, an unsupportive husband, and no parents to lean back on, but she kept climbing. She knew her why, and that carried through with every new position she took. Her "why" was helping people, whether she was doing that at someone's bedside or by changing the way emergency departments are run. She began her career as a nurse, and she slowly achieved new management and leadership positions that ultimately led her to the corporate office at Wellstar. Your why will prove to be your motivation -- the reason you want to succeed. You will do what you set out to do whether it is to help one person or to change the world.

Dr. Melissa Rhodes gives amazing advice on how to learn from our failures:

> "You may fail, we can learn from our failures. None of us are perfect. And if we can, if we try again, the next time we may be better, and we may not make that mistake. I make mistakes, and I try to learn from those mistakes, instead of just saying 'I failed.' Try to learn from mistakes and take every failure and turn it around as a positive because everyday we can learn from our failures and from our successes."

When dealing with what seems like failure, do not be overly critical of yourself. Freda Lyon told me about instances where she would see a male with less experience and qualifications receive jobs instead of more qualified female candidates. Even though it was unfair, she did not let this unfair system affect her. She knew that, although this less-experienced man failed at his job, the extra time and experience she was able to gain made her more prepared for the job which she may not have been ready for at the time. Seeing failure as an opportunity is the path to success.

In contrast, fear of failure is one of the biggest mistakes you can make. To get stronger, you must fail a few times first. Jill Rowley explained this simple analogy: when working out at the gym to build muscular strength, you need to do high-intensity weights. Although you were using a seven-pound weight yesterday, today you should use an eight-pound one to challenge yourself, even if you cannot complete all the reps. To get stronger, you need to push your body further than you have before so you slowly build muscular strength and endurance. Similarly, when embarking on a new task, it is okay not to succeed the first time. By trying again, you will grow stronger until you can overcome whatever obstacle is in your way.

Do not be afraid to fail. You define the response to failure. It may be a reason to quit or an opportunity to try again. Your mindset in this regard will help determine your future. By valuing your mistakes, you allow yourself so much room to grow and succeed. Find your why and let that lead you to success. Allow yourself to learn from each mistake and grow as a person from it. Each mistake does not define you, but how you react to it does. So use each mistake as a learning opportunity, and if you do that, each failure will lead to even greater success.

Thank You

As we begin our professional journeys, the experiences and stories from these female leaders can help guide our progress, allowing us to learn from their successes, failures, achievements, and mistakes. Take their advice and lessons as a learning tool and use it to build your future. These women want to see you succeed, and they hope that you are part of the next generation of female leaders. Throughout your journey, there will be many people who want to see you succeed, and they will offer their advice, time, and money to see that through. Hold those relationships close to your heart because you will learn more from them than you will in the classroom. They will help through your hardest times, making you stronger and more prepared for your next challenge.

Do not doubt yourself. You already have everything that you need to succeed. Allow yourself to explore and learn and grow. Think of the possibilities and the promises of the future, and grab every opportunity that comes your way. At the same time, do not be afraid to seek out and fight for the opportunities that you want. You are in charge of your own future, so live your life in the driver's seat. Prioritize the places *you* want to visit, strive for the school that *you* want to attend, and pursue the path that *you* want to follow. Do not ignore your own ambitions and challenge yourself to be the best version of yourself.

You are the next generation of scientists, doctors, cooks, lawyers, caregivers, entrepreneurs, nurses, executives, and leaders. You are following the footsteps of the women who have hiked the mountain in front of you, and you are paving a path for those who follow. As a young girl, your creative and eager mind can help you to immerse yourself in education, culture, and your future. The world is so vast and filled with infinite opportunities. Step outside your comfort zone to experience a few of the many possibilities. In the process, you may discover a passion that you did not know existed.

Ultimately, you define success for yourself. For many of the female leaders, success was the same as happiness. For others, it came from how much they have helped others and given back. Explaining her definition of success, Jana Kolarik says, "It does not have anything to do with money. It does not have anything to do with having a powerful position. It has more to do with being happy and passionate about what you do, no matter what that is, enjoyment and passion, and helping people." Although success is subjective, it most often does not relate to money or power, but instead to happiness. All the female leaders featured in the book are not just successful for their career prowess. Rather, they are happy with what they do. Find something you love, so whenever you work, you are fueled by passion and work hard to fulfill your goals.

Find the people who support you and are there to help

you rise. The family, friends, and mentors that help guide you will remain a part of your story for the rest of your life, and their advice will remain in your head. At times, you may feel indescribably alone, but always remember that people are here to support you. As the old adage reminds us, light shines brightest in the darkness, so in all circumstances, let your light shine. You are talented and brilliant, and, as long as you continue to work hard, you will be able to do anything you put your mind to.

It is never too early to start building your foundation. Today, you did that by reading this book, and tomorrow, continue building it in a different way. The love of learning and the love of reading will open your mind up to infinite possibilities to show you everything you can be.

Always be yourself. There is only one you, and the world needs you, not whoever you may be pretending to be. Your thoughts, personality, and destiny are unique and beautiful.

People want to see your ideas and your passion, not anyone else's. Do not be afraid to stand out because, when you do stand out, you will be noticed.

Thank you for taking the time to read my work, and I hope these women have inspired you as much as they inspired me. In the end, I hope that you leave this book knowing that you are capable of so much. I hope to see you in the future, living your definition of success and leading the world to be a better place.

Printed in the United States
By Bookmasters